Blessings,

Pastor Kente

LEADING GOD'S WAY

Kevin S. Lee

CROSSBOOKS
PUBLISHING

CrossBooks™
A Division of LifeWay
1663 Liberty Drive
Bloomington, IN 47403
www.crossbooks.com
Phone: 1-866-879-0502

Requests for information should be addressed to:
ReachforLife, P.O. Box 4371, Mountain View, Ca. 94040
www.reachforlifecommunity.com

First published by CrossBooks 10/4/2013

ISBN: 978-1-4627-3156-5 (sc)
ISBN: 978-1-4627-3157-2 (e)

Printed in the United States of America.

This book is printed on acid-free paper.

TABLE OF CONTENTS

DEDICATION

This book is dedicated to my biological father, Donald P. Lee, and my spiritual father, Pastor Paul E. Sheppard. Over many years, you have led, influenced, and challenged me to be great. I truly appreciate the role you have played in my life. We have just one biological father and not many spiritual fathers. I praise God for you! You have helped me become the man I am today. Now, I am a young Joshua **Leading God's Way** for the next generation.

WELCOME TO THE LEADING GOD'S WAY BIBLE STUDY SERIES

The world is made up of two kinds of people; those who like shape, order and frameworks, and those who prefer to work in an open, free-ranging, spontaneous style. This book is for people who like shape, order, and frameworks.

It's great to be open, free-ranging, and spontaneous. God often works in the life of Christian believers who are open to His will for their life. Daily we must rely on and trust the Holy Spirit to work on our behalf. We must be sensitive and ever ready to experience God when He shows up unexpectedly and wants to bless us. To be sure, to experience God is to know Him more fully! But it's also helpful to put our Christian faith into a recognizable shape, something that can act as a kind of checklist to make sure we are guided, reminded, growing and continuing to move forward.

It is very easy to have wonderfully good intentions, but often times we can actually find ourselves drifting slowly downstream and feeling incapable of paddling back to shore against the strong currents (i.e., distractions) of life. At times, we become tempted to miss a time of prayer or Bible reading. We might be tempted to miss Sunday worship, an opportunity to give, or an opportunity to serve the body of Christ. We say to ourselves, "Well, I can miss just this once. God understands." This is all too common for many believers in the Christian church. Over time though we end up spending more time focused on our self and less time with God.

Maybe you decide to go to church every week you're at home, but if you are away on a road trip or at school you only go if it fits the particular situation. Maybe you pray with your family every morning before you leave for work and at every Sunday worship service, but you do not make time to pray during the other days of the week. Maybe you decide to attend a Bible study on Monday and Wednesday, but you only make it to church 2 to 3 times a month. Maybe you serve or give when it's convenient for you, but not according to biblical principles. We must closely examine our lives to determine if we are truly **Leading God's Way** or if we are putting our own selfish needs before God.

So what follows is what I call Leadership Guideposts, which means important keys of spiritual life designed to guard and guide our good intentions. These guideposts are some core fundamentals that all men and women must embody if they profess to be leaders in the Christian church. The key guideposts to **Leading God's Way** are *leading* others, *studying* God's Word, *serving* God and others, *giving* to the Kingdom, *worshipping* the Almighty, and *praying* regularly.

This study series will help you as you dig into the Word because deep down inside every Christian believer wants to be a stronger, more effective, leader who grows closer to God everyday. We human beings don't enjoy living our life when we aren't living an authentic lifestyle, especially when it comes to serving in a leadership role. We are not happy when we know we are not fulfilling the calling He has on our life. We desire to be authentic leaders who are *doers of the Word*, but many of us seek to spend more time walking in a worldly realm filled with family responsibilities, work, sports, and other things that compete for our time with God rather than spending time 'going deep and getting deep' in the things of God.

There are many resources and tools available to help believers grow everyday. This book aims to help believers - young, old, new, and experienced – grow and become better leaders. If these lessons reach you, I pray that **Leading God's Way** would help you renew your commitment to live an authentic Christian life and be the leader God has destined you to be.

HOW TO USE THIS STUDY GUIDE

As you begin this study, read the short **Study Start** and **Study Goals**, which will help you to focus before you 'dig in.' You can discuss as a group or in separate break out groups whether you will add more goals to your study. The **Digging In Deeper** section is designed for you to do just that...dig in deeper to God's Word. Consider this section to be your homework prior to the group meeting. This will assure that everyone is well prepared for the small group session and well equipped to share intimate knowledge of the Word and personal application.

When the small group comes together, you should be able to read the **Digging In Deeper** questions aloud and invite each member to share what s/he learned and what God has spoken to each person's heart. The group leader may invite new insights, personal sharing, questions, concerns, and comments that have arisen during the personal study of each member over the past week. Everyone should have an opportunity to share to maximize the most from each person's study time. If your group is too large (10 or more members), you may want to break out into smaller groups (three to four) so that each individual can get the maximum benefit of the study.

Next, move onto **Accountability Check In**, which offers some challenging questions about your personal life. This section gets at the heart of where you are personally on a particular topic and challenges you to be honest with yourself. The group leader can read the questions aloud and each member can respond to the degree s/he feels comfortable sharing. The group leader can facilitate the interaction to keep the discussion moving.

Accountability Check In will be followed by **Group Discussion**, which will provide a broader array of questions that the group can interact with. You should leave time, depending on what the group decides, to practice the **Memorization Verse**. Should you decide to commit key verses to memory be prepared for God's Word to sink deep into your heart. This is a great goal because your study will take you places you could never imagine.

Don't forget to leave time for **KeyPoints** and **Lifelines**. These sections will help you reinforce what you've already learned. As you begin to digest what you've already taken in, the **KeyPoints** will reinforce this information and the Lifelines will give you the 'How To' so you can start to live out God's Word everyday.

Finally, you will work the **Group Exercises** to practice what you've learned. God will test you to see if you have learned the lesson He is trying to show you. This section will bring everything together. The group leader can invite each member to add their own exercise or add any concluding points of personal sharing that will benefit the group. The group leader should end each session with prayer and invite others to join to thank God for His goodness.

In review, the general format for each session is:
- Study Start
- Study Goals
- Digging In Deeper
- Accountability Check In
- Group Discussion
- Memorization Verse
- KeyPoints
- Lifelines
- Group Exercises

I hope you enjoy **Leading God's Way!**

LEADING GOD'S WAY

LEADERS LEAD OTHERS

STUDY START

We have different gifts, according to the grace given to each of us. If your gift is prophesying, then prophesy in accordance with your faith; if it is serving, then serve; if it is teaching, then teach; if it is to encourage, then give encouragement; if it is giving, then give generously; if it is to <u>lead</u>, do it diligently; if it is to show mercy, do it cheerfully.[1]

The Bible doesn't explicitly tell us much about leadership. In fact, we find only a limited number of occurrences of the word "lead" or some variation thereof in all the pages of Scripture.[2] Despite these limited references, you probably still have an idea of some leadership qualities that come to mind when you think about what leadership looks like for your boss, spouse, parent, coach, or some other person in a leadership role.

But, what do you think about when you think of Christian leadership? What are some of the characteristics of the person in a leadership role? The Bible gives us some examples of Christian leadership. The best example is found in the words of Jesus Christ who declared, "I am the good shepherd. The good shepherd lays down his life for the sheep."[3] In this verse, we see the best description of a Christian leader. He is one who shepherds and sacrifices all for the "sheep" under his care.[4]

When Jesus used the word "sheep" he was referring to us and it was not meant as a compliment because sheep rank among the lowest in intelligence of all animals in creation. When a sheep strays from the herd, but is still near by, that sheep becomes frightened, confused, and unable to find its way back to the flock. The stray also becomes unprotected and susceptible to harm by predators roaming nearby.

What Christ meant was that without a shepherd, we are helpless. The leader is one who leads, feeds, nurtures, comforts, corrects and protects the flock. The shepherd of God's flock leads by modeling godliness in his own life and encouraging others to follow his example. Without a shadow of doubt, the ultimate example of leadership is Christ Himself. He is the example we should follow. The Apostle Paul understood this: "Follow my example, as I follow the example of Christ."[5] The Christian leader ought to follow Christ and encourage others, by his example, to do the same.[6]

The Christian leader feeds the flock through God's Word. The Bible is the only diet that can produce healthy Christians. "... man does not live on bread alone but on every word that comes from the mouth of the Lord."[7] The Christian leader comforts the sheep and binds up their wounds through application of God's compassion and love. The Lord will "bind up the injured and strengthen the weak."[8] The Christian leader corrects and disciplines those in his flock when they wander away. The Lord disciplines those he loves[9] and the Christian leader must follow His example, but not with an overbearing spirit, but with a "spirit of gentleness."[10]

The Christian leader protects the sheep from predators; (i.e., teachers of false doctrine). Jesus warned us: "Watch out for false prophets. They come to you in sheep's clothing, but inwardly they are ferocious wolves."[11] Today's leaders must protect us from the false teachings of those who would lead us astray from the truth of the Scripture and the fact that Christ alone is the way of salvation: "I am the way, the truth, and the life. No one comes to the Father except through me."[12]

Those whom God calls as leaders are not to rule with a heavy hand, but rather as humble servants. Those who would lead God's people must above all exude sacrifice, devotion, submission, and lowliness. Jesus Himself gave us the pattern when He washed His disciples' feet, a task that was customarily done by the lowest of slaves.[13] If the God of all creation would do that how much more should we imitate our Heavenly father.

We must be leaders who decide that the only way to lead is **Leading God's Way**, not leaning on our own understanding.[14] God has unique plans for us as Christian leaders.[15] He wants us to submit to his leading in every area of our life. He wants us to submit in every area of leadership.[16] When we surrender and follow His lead He takes us on a journey unlike none we have ever experienced. The result of **Leading God's Way** is peace that surpasses all understanding, overwhelming prosperity, unlimited blessings, and unspeakable joy!

STUDY GOALS

Goals for this lesson:

1. Learn more about leadership style as it relates to biblical leadership

2. Learn more about how I should serve as a Christian leader

3. Learn more about my own strengths and weaknesses as a leader

4. Learn how to serve like Christ in my leadership role(s)

DIGGING IN DEEPER

Read Romans 12:6-8

We have different gifts, according to the grace given to each of us. If your gift is prophesying, then prophesy in accordance with your faith; if it is serving, then serve; if it is teaching, then teach; if it is to encourage, then give encouragement; if it is giving, then give generously; if it is to lead, do it diligently; if it is to show mercy, do it cheerfully.[17]

1. Pray. Read the passage again. Tell God that you want to be obedient to whatever He reveals to you about your leadership role(s). Ask the Holy Spirit to guide your thoughts about leadership.

2. Now, look a bit closer and study the passage. Make sure you observe the words and phrases.

    a. What does the passage reveal about leading? Leadership?

b. Is there anything that comes to mind that you did not recognize before? If so, write down your thoughts.

c. Use your Bible and a commentary to determine the context of the passage? What comes before and after?

d. What do you know about Paul's circumstances at the time he wrote the letter?

e. Use a concordance to look up additional verses or key phrases.

3. Reflect. Take some time to think about what you've read. Do you have any new or different thoughts?

4. Journal Writing. Write out a short summary of your 'take aways' from the passage. How does what you've learned apply in your life?

PRAYER & ACCOUNTABILITY CHECK-IN

1. Have you submitted every area of your life to God? Every area? Every area of leadership?

2. Do you place the needs of others before your own in your leadership role(s)?

3. Do you bring all our thoughts to God in prayer and ask Him for His direction concerning every leadership decision?

4. Is there anything in your life hindering you from being an effective leader? Personal issue? Idol? Other?

5. Pray and ask God to help you be the best leader. Ask him to help you with you weaknesses/shortcomings. Pray for His direction, discernment, guidance, and wisdom.

GROUP DISCUSSION

1. What are some important qualities that all leaders should possess? Christian leaders?

2. List some of the best leaders you have known (alive or deceased). What makes the leader(s) you mentioned a great leader? Do they have weaknesses or shortcomings? Explain.

3. Who do you believe is the best contemporary leader? What makes that person a great leader?

4. Do you think we have a leadership problem today? Locally? Nationally? Internationally?

5. If you believe that there is a leadership problem today what do you believe is the solution?

6. Should we continue to dialogue about leadership or is the subject no longer vogue and/or worthy of discussion?

MEMORY VERSE:

"I am the good shepherd. The good shepherd lays down his life for the sheep"[18]

KeyPoints:

1. Prayer will bring us to a place of peace when we surrender everything to God and ask Him to meet us where we are.

2. A Christian believer is a servant who places the needs of others before himself in his leadership role(s).

3. We should bring all our thoughts to God in prayer and ask Him for direction concerning every leadership decision.

Lifelines:

1. Understand the importance of servant leadership.

2. Be a leader who serves with honesty and integrity.

3. Bring all of your decisions before God in prayer.

4. It's imperative that every believer serves like Christ.

GROUP EXERCISES

1. What are the greatest challenges you face as a leader? You don't feel confident? You don't feel secure in your role? You feel overwhelmed? You don't manage your time well? You feel it's more of an obligation and you don't want to commit? Share your challenges with the group. What do you suppose others in leadership have, or do, or get that you don't?

2. Using your Note Pages, write down ways in which you can overcome some of the leadership challenges you experience.

3. Locate and share with the group some scripture verses that are helpful to you regarding your leadership role(s). Each person in the group should commit at least one verse to memory.

4. Individual Exercise: Make up a list of leadership do's and don'ts (use your Note Pages) based on your experience. Share your list with the group.

5. Individual Exercise: Share with the group some books and resources that you have found helpful to supplement your Bible reading and have helped you grow your leadership skills.

LEADERS STUDY
GOD'S WORD

STUDY START

"For the Word of God is living and active and sharper than any two-edged sword, and piercing as far as the division of soul and spirit, of both joints and marrow, and able to judge the thoughts and intentions of the heart."[19]

Why must Christian believers turn to the Bible for instruction? Because Jesus Himself said, "It is written: Man does not live on bread alone, but on every word that comes from the mouth of God."[20] Christ's words come in the form of command. It's only through the words of God, and no other means, delivered by his human vessels[21] that bring shape and form to the power of God that we must encounter for salvation and renewal of our soul. It's only through God's awesome power[22] that we are purified and enabled to grow spiritually[23] to withstand the lure of sin. The Word of God is a living power that is manifested in our lives by the Holy Spirit, as we first trust, then rely upon the Spirit to shape our lives.[24] For all the wonderful advice we get from Godly men and women, for all the great preaching we receive from great Bible teaching pastors, for the many how-to books we read to help improve our everyday life, for all the positive things we endeavor to do to grow, nothing can ever match the power of God's Word to enable us to grow from infant to mature believer.

The process of Bible study begins as we approach Scripture daily with prayer – asking God to reveal Himself to us. We approach the text seeking to grow in our spiritual understanding that we might comprehend doctrine that equips, purifies and perfects those who ardently pursue it.[25] As we approach the Bible to interpret and apply God's Word to our lives, we ask Him to remove any barriers that might hinder our understanding and enable us to adopt His mind (a mind of Christ) so that we might fully appreciate our relationship with Him and other people. As we sink ourselves into the text we anticipate the opportunity to root ourselves deeper in true Christian morality.[26] The hope and goal is that we might become wiser, stronger, more discerning, conscientious and more zealous for God than ever before. The hope and goal is living our life as a 'walking epistle' as we maintain a heavenly focus and one-day attaining *perfection in Christ.*

Below is an easy systematic approach to help you begin studying your Bible. This approach can be applied to a verse-by-verse study, a passage study, or an entire book. Before you begin, pray and ask God to help you uncover the text and discover the author's originally intended meaning so that you can deepen your personal walk with Christ. Remember, this is about adding depth to your personal relationship with God so He needs to hear from you and you from Him. The Father already knows who you are. He knows every intimate detail about your life. He knows the number of hairs on your head.[27] Now is your chance to know His character, His power, His sorrows, and His heart.

First, choose a passage. If you don't already have one in mind, you might want to consider any of the following: John 15:4, Hebrews 12:1 or Acts 1:8.

There are three important components to studying your Bible for understanding:

Observation –Read through a particular passage and begin to make general observations about the text you are reading.

Observe what comes before the text and what follows the verses or passage you selected. Make some notes to yourself about the "who, what, when, and where" of the passage. Make a note of every word in the passage because every word is important. Every word in the Bible is God's Word. Notice words that are repeated and phrases that jump out. Try to list some of the most obvious things you notice and try to make at least 10-20 observations. Feel free to use a dictionary to define key words to help bring clarity to your understanding. Observe different parts of speech (i.e., verb tense) to help you understand what the author is trying to convey to his audience. Finally, observe the passage in the context of the book and the Bible as a whole.[28]

Interpretation —Second, you will begin to interpret the passage. This is where you clarify the meaning of the passage and gain insight why the Holy Spirit included this passage in Scripture. You will seek to answer the question, "What does it mean?" In this step, you will interpret the passage based on grammatical, historical, and cultural aspects of the text. You will explore the literary context (narrative, poetry, other) and historical context (background and setting), and the cultural aspect of society at the time the text was written. At this stage, you may compare scripture passages from other portions of Scripture and relate the passage from the rest of the book and Bible as a whole. The goal is to study diligently in order to transport yourself back in time to discover the author's originally intended meaning of the text to help you know what the passage means for your life today.[29]

Application —Finally, you will apply the passage to your life.[30] This is where you will want to listen closely to what the Holy Spirit has been pointing out to you as you have been reading and studying the passage. You may want to review your notes again to glean more about how this passage personally applies to you. Are you able to pick up on some themes or threads connected to what you've written down? There may be some messages there that God has for you, but He wants you to look closely so that you can gain new insight from His Word. Write down any thoughts or insights you gain from further study. Ask yourself some questions: Is there some sin that I need to avoid? Is there a promise from God for me to claim? Is there an example for me to follow? Is there a commandment for me to obey? How can this passage increase my knowledge of God the Father, the son Jesus Christ, and the Holy Spirit? What is God showing me about myself? Most importantly, write down a personal and specific application for you, not someone else. Pray and ask God to help you apply what you've learned so that you can be at the center of His will.

STUDY GOALS

Goals for this lesson:

1. Learn how to study God's Word

2. Learn how to get deeper into the Word

3. Learn how to interpret and understand the Word

4. Learn how God's Word applies to your life

DIGGING IN DEEPER

Salvation through Jesus Christ is the main topic in the New Testament. The Bible covers topics relating to salvation, sin, repentance, forgiveness, and others that help provide biblical guidance for Christians to follow. Review the passages below and try to determine how each passage relates to salvation.

Matthew 8:18-22

Matthew 19:25-26

Romans 3:8

Romans 3:23

Romans 8:38-39

Romans 10:9-10

Philippians 3:4-11

Isaiah 57:12

Luke 3:8

Hebrews 7:25

Revelation 22:17

PRAYER & ACCOUNTABILITY CHECK-IN

1. Have you read the entire Bible? If not, how much have you read? How much Bible reading do you complete daily? Weekly? Explain.

2. How do you read your Bible? Do you use supplemental tools? If so, share some of the tools you use.

3. Do you pray before you read your Bible? Do you ask God to remove any and all hindrances so He can reveal Himself to you through the Word?

4. Is there anything in your life hindering you from hearing from God? Personal issue? Idol? Other?

5. Pray and ask God for guidance before, during, and after you read the Bible. Ask him to help you see your weaknesses/ shortcomings. Pray that God would reveal Himself to you while you read His Word.

GROUP DISCUSSION

1. Is there a particular passage or verse in Scripture that has caused you to avoid sin or has brought you under conviction in your life? Explain.

2. List some of the promises you claim from Scripture and share them with the group. Why are those promises important to you?

3. Name some important examples (i.e., Christ) that we can follow from the pages of Scripture. Share them with the group. How are you following biblical examples in your life?

4. Share several commandments found in the Bible. Are they hard to follow? Impossible? Why should we follow God's commandments? Are there any commandments we shouldn't follow?

5. Share how God's Word has changed your life? How has the Bible shaped and molded your daily walk with Jesus Christ? Explain.

6. Did you recently learn something new about the Bible that you didn't know before? How much time do you spend studying God's Word each week?

7. What does your Bible study look like? Share with the group. How can you improve your study time alone with God?

MEMORIZATION VERSE

For the Word of God is living and active and sharper than any two-edged sword, and piercing as far as the division of soul and spirit, of both joints and marrow, and able to judge the thoughts and intentions of the heart.[31]

KeyPoints

1. When we get into God's Word He gets into us.

2. Begin studying the Word by praying and observing.

3. We must ask the Holy Spirit to help us understand the Bible.

4. We must apply God's Word in our life everyday.

Lifelines

1. Seek God in prayer and ask Him to reveal Himself through the Word.

2. Review and memorize the scripture passages you read in your daily study.

3. Join a Bible study group to help you grow in your understanding and application of God's Word.

4. Read your Bible regularly. Make it your top priority to grow with God everyday.

GROUP EXERCISES

1. Reading Life Review: A review of your study life is an excellent way to begin the process of developing a study strategy. By examining what is happening or not happening, it is possible to identify ways of encouraging further growth in what is already going on, and also spotting the "gaps." Here are some questions to consider. Where is the best place for you to study? What is the best time of day? How much time can you spend reading the Bible? 10 minutes? 20 minutes? 45 minutes? 1 hour? How should you study during your Bible reading time? By verse? Chapter? Topic? Share your responses and challenges with the group. What do you suppose those with a more fulfilled study life have, or do, or get that you don't?

2. Develop a Strategy: Develop a strategy for regular Bible study. A study strategy is typically a short document, possibly only with a few bullet points, that outlines how you plan to develop your Bible reading life, and ensure that your reading needs are adequately covered. Develop your own personal study strategy by writing several specific bullet points on a sheet of paper (perhaps on your Note Pages) that will help you spend more time in God's Word. Feel free to discuss the areas of greatest personal challenge with the group so others can help you accomplish your goal(s).

3. Locate and share with the group some Bible verses or passages that you have spent time recently studying to gain a deeper understanding of God's Word. Each person in the group should share at least one verse or passage to explain to the group.

4. Individual Exercise: Share regularly with your group how you are doing with regard to meeting the goals you have set in your Bible study strategy. Are you 'hit and miss?' Are you consistently meeting your goal(s)? What is most challenging

for you? Share what your personal daily experience is like while you're reading God's Word.

5. Individual Exercise: Share with the group some books and resources that you have found helpful to supplement your Bible reading. To the extent you are able, locate some new tools to help enhance your intimacy with God.

LEADERS SERVE GOD AND OTHERS

STUDY START

"For even the Son of Man did not come to be served, but to serve, and to give his life as a ransom for many."[32]

Is it really necessary to serve God? Does God really need us to help him? Why should we change our priorities when God can honestly do what He wants to do better and faster without us?

The apostle Peter speaks to the importance of serving God when he says that each one should use whatever gift he has received to serve others, faithfully administering God's grace in its various forms. If anyone speaks, he should do it as one speaking the very words of God.[33] If any serves, he should do it with the strength God provides, so that in all things God may be praised through Jesus Christ. To him are the glory and the power forever and ever. Amen."[34]

Peter makes it plain that we have received our gifts from God for two reasons – to serve others and to bring glory to God. Serving is not about you or me getting any glory. It's all about God getting glory!

Does God really get glory when we serve? Well, the answer to this question is pretty straightforward. The transforming power of Jesus Christ is displayed in the lives of those who have given over selfishness for selflessness. Peter says that believers should recognize that we are speaking and serving directly on behalf of

God to others, while He gives the ability and strength for us to do so. And when we direct glory towards Him instead of accepting it ourselves, we stand out from the crowd of those who glorify only themselves. And that difference in our lives causes people to examine the life-changing nature of a relationship with Jesus Christ. It bears witness to our faith for all to see.

Why should I serve God? Well, it's not just important and selfless, but it's a believer's job while here on earth. How do we know that for sure? Well, Paul tells us in Romans 12:1-2: "Therefore, I urge you, brothers, in view of God's mercy, to offer your bodies as living sacrifices, holy and pleasing to God—this is your spiritual act of worship.[35] Do not conform any longer to the pattern of this world, but be transformed by the renewing of your mind. Then you will be able to test and approve what God's will is—his good, pleasing and perfect will."[36]

Paul tells us that serving is for those who have been saved by the blood of Jesus so it only makes sense to honor God.[37] Since God has been so kind to us, meaning He hasn't executed His wrath and allowed us to stay alive, then it only makes sense for us to serve Him. Further, and equally importantly, serving is our spiritual act of worship (the Greek word for "spiritual" can also be translated "reasonable"). It's the reason why God created us and it's the reason we are on the planet. We are here to worship Him! Thus, it's only reasonable that we'd serve the Lord who has provided the greatest service of all: salvation from sin and eternal life with Him in heaven.

STUDY GOALS

Goals for this lesson:

1. Understand what it means to serve God

2. Learn more about how we ought to serve God

3. Understand what the Bible tells us about serving God

DIGGING IN DEEPER

Review the Bible verses listed below and try to determine how each verse relates to serving or how we should serve God.

"Only fear the Lord and serve him faithfully with all your heart. For consider what great things he has done for you." (1 Sam. 12:24)

"I appeal to you therefore, brothers, by the mercies of God, to present your bodies as a living sacrifice, holy and acceptable to God, which is your spiritual worship." (Rom. 12:1)

"Each one must give as he has decided in his heart, not reluctantly or under compulsion, for God loves a cheerful giver." (2 Cor. 9:7)

"But you are a chosen race, a royal priesthood, a holy nation, a people for his own possession, that you may proclaim the excellencies of him who called you out of darkness into his marvelous light." (1 Pet. 2:9)

"Therefore, my beloved brothers, be steadfast, immovable, always abounding in the work of the Lord, knowing that in the Lord your labor is not in vain." (1 Cor. 15:58)

"And you, Solomon my son, know the God of your father and serve him with a whole heart and with a willing mind, for the Lord searches all hearts and understands every plan and thought. If you seek him, he will be found by you, but if you forsake him, he will cast you off forever." (1 Chron. 28:9)

"No one can serve two masters, for either he will hate the one and love the other, or he will be devoted to the one and despise the other. You cannot serve God and money. (Matt. 6:24)

"But lay up for yourselves treasures in heaven, where neither moth nor rust destroys and where thieves do not break in and steal. For where your treasure is, there your heart will be also. "The eye is the lamp of the body. So, if your eye is healthy, your whole body will be full of light, but if your eye is bad, your whole body will be full of darkness. If then the light in you is darkness, how great is the darkness! "No one can serve two masters, for either he will hate the one and love the other, or he will be devoted to the one and despise the other. You cannot serve God and money." (Matt. 6:20-24)

"Let no one despise you for your youth, but set the believers an example in speech, in conduct, in love, in faith, in purity." (1 Tim. 4:12)

"Religion that is pure and undefiled before God, the Father, is this: to visit orphans and widows in their affliction, and to keep oneself unstained from the world." (Jas. 1:27)

"For the kingdom of heaven is like a master of a house who went out early in the morning to hire laborers for his vineyard. After agreeing with the laborers for a denarius a day, he sent them into his vineyard. And going out about the third hour he saw others standing idle in the marketplace, and to them he said, 'You go into the vineyard too, and whatever is right I will give you.' So they went. Going out again about the sixth hour and the ninth hour, he did the same...." (Matt. 20:1-16)

"For he will hide me in his shelter in the day of trouble; he will conceal me under the cover of his tent; he will lift me high upon a rock." (Ps. 27:5)

"This Book of the Law shall not depart from your mouth, but you shall meditate on it day and night, so that you may be careful to do according to all that is written in it. For then you will make your way prosperous, and then you will have good success." (Jos. 1:8)

PRAYER & ACCOUNTABILITY CHECK-IN

1. Have you ever washed someone's feet? How do you serve others? What does serving look like to you?

2. Do you place the needs of others before your own as a servant of God? If so, share examples how?

3. Do you bring all your thoughts to God in prayer and ask Him for direction concerning every servant leadership decision?

4. Is there anything in your life hindering you from being an effective servant of God? Personal issue(s)? Idol? Other?

5. Pray and ask God to help you be the best servant. Ask him to help you with your weaknesses/shortcomings. Pray for His direction, discernment, guidance, and wisdom.

GROUP DISCUSSION

1. Is there a particular passage or verse in Scripture that has helped you understand what it means to serve God? Explain.

2. List some of the ways you serve in the church or elsewhere and share them with your group. What are your favorite ways to serve? Least favorite? Why?

3. Name some important examples of serving that we can follow from the pages of Scripture. Share them with the group. How are you following biblical examples in your life? Can you be better? If so, how?

4. Share one or two stories about how and where you have served God? Mission trip? Elsewhere? Feel free to share both positive and negative experiences. How has serving God influenced your life?

5. How can you improve your serve?

6. Did you learn something new in this study about serving God that you didn't know before? How much time do you spend serving God each day? Week? Month? Can you give God more time?

MEMORIZATION VERSE

For even the Son of Man did not come to be served, but to serve, and to give his life as a ransom for many."[38]

KeyPoints

1. Serving others isn't about us; it's about glorifying God.

2. Everyday is a good opportunity to improve your serve.

3. God created us to serve. We are here on earth to serve our Creator.

4. It's only reasonable that we serve God because He saved us from sin.

Lifelines

1. God loves you and He created you to serve Him everyday.

2. Review and internalize the scripture passages that were covered in this study.

3. Regularly serve in a church ministry. If applicable, teach your young children about serving. We serve God through serving others.

4. Serve God because He is great and His love endures forever.

GROUP EXERCISES

1. Talk about serving in the church? Where do you serve? Why do you serve in that particular area of ministry? What steps did you take before you started serving? A course? A conversation?

2. Using your Note Pages, write down different ways in which you serve God on Sunday or throughout the week. List all the ways that you believe you regularly serve God.

3. Identify and share key scripture verses about serving that you have found helpful. Each person in the group should share at least one verse.

4. Individual Exercise: Make up a strategy list (write it on your Note Pages) how you believe you can improve your serve. To the extent you feel comfortable, share it with the group.

5. Individual Exercise: Share with the group some books and resources that have helped to enlighten you about serving. To the extent you are able, locate some new tools to help enhance your spiritual growth.

LEADERS GIVE TO THE KINGDOM

STUDY START

"Remember this: Whoever sows sparingly will also reap sparingly, and whoever sows generously will also reap generously. Each man should give what he has decided in his heart to give, not reluctantly or under compulsion, for God loves a cheerful giver."[39]

The way we give to God is an indication of our love for Him. Everything belongs to God. God says in Psalms 50:10, "For every beast of the forest is mine, and the cattle on a thousand hills."[40] Everything we have received has come from God. God has only loaned them to us. John 3:27 says, "A man can receive nothing unless it has been given to him from above."[41] We can never out-give God. In Luke 6:38 we read, "Give, and it shall be given unto you; good measure, pressed down, shaken together, and running over, shall men give into your bosom. For with the same measure that you use, it will be measured back to you."[42] We give so that God's church can better carry out its mission here on earth. The world must be evangelized, and the church must be lifted, and the needy must be helped.

Giving is a command of the Lord. In 1 Corinthians 16:1-2 we read, "Now about the collections for the Lord's people: Do what I told the Galatian churches to do. On the first day of every week, each one of you should set aside a sum of money in keeping with your income saving it up, so that when I come no collections will have to be made."[43] We see that giving in this context was to help the poor saints in Jerusalem. Notice also they were to make a regular collection every first day of the week.[44]

Because of everything God has given us, including Christ's death on the cross, we should be anxious to give back to Him. In 2 Corinthians 8:12 we read, "For if the willingness is there, the gift is acceptable according to what one has, not according to what one doesn't not have."[45] God expects us to give what we are able to give. How can our love for God be genuine unless it is expressed in our obedience and our giving? Our giving is an expression of love and an act of praise to glorify to God.

How we give is an indication of where our priorities are. Jesus says in Matthew 6:19-21, "Do not lay up for yourselves treasures on earth, where moth and rust destroy and where thieves break in and steal. But store up for yourselves treasures in heaven, where neither moth and rust destroys and where thieves do not break in and steal. For where your treasure is, there will your heart be also."[46] Where is your heart?

Since we cannot out-give God, we should at least be liberal in our giving. As we read in 2 Corinthians 9:6-7, "Remember this: Whoever sows sparingly will also reap sparingly, and whoever sows generously will reap generously. Each of you should give what you have decided in your heart to give, not reluctantly or under compulsion, for God loves a cheerful giver."[47] Our giving is to be carefully planned. We should not give out of compulsion or resentment. These are not the right motives to give to God. We should be glad that we can give to the Lord.

We should never try to impress other people with our giving. Giving needs to be a private matter. We should not seek recognition for the things we do. Jesus says in Matthew 6:1-4, "Take heed that you do not do your charitable deeds before men, to be seen of them. Otherwise you have no reward from your Father in heaven. Therefore, when you do a charitable deed, do not sound a trumpet before you as the hypocrites do in the synagogues and in the streets, that they may have glory from men. Assuredly, I say to you, they have their reward. But when you do a charitable deed, do not let your left hand know what your right hand is doing, that your charitable deed may be in secret; and your Father who sees in secret will Himself reward you openly."[48] We should seek the approval of God, not the glory of men.

Our giving should not only include material possessions but we must first give ourselves to God. We are told in Romans 12:1, "I beseech you therefore, brethren, by the mercies of God, that you present your bodies a living sacrifice, holy, acceptable to God, which is your reasonable service."[49] If we will first give ourselves to God, we will have no problem in being liberal in our giving. Our liberal giving is part of worshipping God "in spirit and in truth."

STUDY GOALS

Goals for this lesson:

1. Learn more about what it means to give to God

2. Learn about different ways you can give to God

3. Learn about being a faithful and generous giver to God

4. Learn about how your giving glorifies God

DIGGING IN DEEPER

PART I. Review the following scripture passages and try to determine how each passage relates to giving.

1. Does God really own everything? (Ps. 24:1; Matt. 25:14; Hag. 2:8)

2. Is there really value in giving to God? (Matt. 6:19-20; 2 Cor. 9:10-11)

3. How should giving fit into your priorities? (Matt. 6:21)

4. What does it mean to give sacrificially? (Gen. 4:4; Mk. 12:41-44; 2 Cor. 9:6; Acts 2:44-45)

5. How should we give to God? (Deut. 16:17; 2 Cor. 9:7)

6. Why do we give to God? (Lk. 6:38; 2 Cor. 9:8, 11)

PART II. TEST – *See if you can pass the test* Review the scripture passages and statements below to determine how, or if, the verse lines up with the applicable statement. Explain.

1. Everything we have we have obtained it ourselves without God's help. (John 3:27)

(Circle One) Some person has given it to us. God has given to us.

2. Nothing we have comes from God.

(Circle One) True. False.

3. When we give we will receive nothing in return from God. (Luke 6:38)

(Circle One) We will receive from God much more than we give.

We will receive very little from God.

4. We can never out give God.

(Circle One) True. False.

5. Giving is: (1 Corinthians 16:1-2)

(Circe One) A command of God.

       Is something we can do if we want.

       It's not a command of God.

6. The Lord's church is to make a regular collection every first day of the week.

(Circle One) True. False.

7. When we give we should: (2 Corinthians 8:12)

(Circle One) Give grudgingly.

       We should give because we have to give.

       We should give willingly.

8. God does not expect us to give because we have already prospered.

(Circle One) True. False.

9. We should lay up our treasures: (Matthew 6:19-21)

(Circle One) In Heaven. On the earth. In the bank.

10. If our treasure is in Heaven, our heart will be there also.

(Circle One) True. False.

11. God loves: (2 Corinthians 9:6-7)

(Circle One) One who does not give.

One who gives grudgingly.

One who gives cheerfully.

12. We should give grudgingly and because we have to.

(Circle One) True. False.

13. How should we do our charitable deeds? (Matthew 6:1-4)

(Circle One) To be seen of men.

For our own glory.

Not to be seen of men.

14. We should give to impress people.

(Circle One) True. False.

15. What should we do for God? (Romans 12:1)

(Circle One) Nothing.

      Give our bodies as a living sacrifice.

      As little as we can.

16. If we first give ourselves to God, we will have no problem with giving liberally.

(Circle One) True. False.

PRAYER & ACCOUNTABILITY CHECK IN

1. Have you submitted every area of your life to God? Your giving?

2. Do you view giving to God as an obligation or an act of worship? Explain.

3. Do you lead your family in giving/tithing to God or do you follow others around you? Explain.

4. Is there anything in your life hindering you from being an effective giver/tither? Explain.

5. Pray and ask God to help you be a better giver/tither. Ask him to help you with your hindrances to giving. Pray for His direction, discernment, guidance, and wisdom.

GENERAL DISCUSSION

1. Are there particular passages or verses in Scripture that have helped you understand what it means to give to God? Explain.

2. List some of the ways you give to God and share them with your group. What are the easiest ways for you to give? Most difficult? Explain.

3. Name some important examples of giving that we find in Scripture. Share them with the group. How are you following biblical examples in your life? Can you be better? If so, how?

4. Share one or two stories about how you have given to God? How has giving to God affected your life? How has God blessed you?

5. How can you improve your giving?

6. Did you learn something new in this study about giving to God that you didn't know before? How much time do you spend giving to God each day? Week? Month? If applicable, can you give more?

MEMORIZATION VERSE

"Remember this: Whoever sows sparingly will also reap sparingly, and whoever sows generously will also reap generously. Each man should give what he has decided in his heart to give, not reluctantly or under compulsion, for God loves a cheerful giver."[50]

KeyPoints

1. God wants us to give to Him with the right heart.

2. We need to ask God to help us if we struggle with giving to Him.

3. We must seek God if we expect to be better givers/tithers.

4. God wants us to give Him our time, talent, and treasure.

Lifelines

1. God rewards those individuals who are faithful and generous givers.

2. Review and memorize scripture passages that were covered in this study.

3. Gain a deeper understanding of giving through regular prayer and Bible study.

4. Give with the right heart and watch how God will bless you and your family.

5. Share your testimony of giving with others so that they will be faithful givers too.

GROUP EXERCISES

1. What are your greatest challenges with regard to giving to God? Share your challenges with the group. What do you suppose those who struggle less in this area of life have, or do, or get that you don't?

2. Using your Note Pages, make a list of your struggle areas with regard to giving to God. Write down some key strategies that can help you overcome the tendency towards not giving as you ought to.

3. Locate and share with the group some scripture verses that are helpful to you with respect to giving. Each person in the group should commit at least one verse to memory.

4. Individual Exercise: Review the Accountability Questions in the back of this book and be honest in your responses. Examine yourself and to the extent you feel comfortable, share with the group.

5. Individual Exercise: Share with the group some books and resources that you have found helpful to supplement your Bible reading. To the extent you are able, locate some new tools to help enhance your daily Christian life.

LEADERS WORSHIP ALMIGHTY GOD

STUDY START

Through Jesus, therefore, let us continually offer to God a sacrifice of praise—the fruit of lips that openly profess his name.[51]

Our worship is to exalt, honor, glorify, praise, and ultimately please God. Our worship must show our loyalty, trust, and adoration to God for He was the one who saved us from our sins. The nature of the worship God requires is that of prostration of our souls before Him, in contrite, humble submission.[52] Our daily worship to God is to be humble and reverent. We serve a wonderful Savior!

God wants us to worship Him in Spirit and truth.[53] The Bible doesn't say we can worship God anyway we want, but we "must worship Him in spirit and in truth."[54] The word "must" makes it absolute. There is no other way we can worship God and glorify Him. The word "must" expresses a necessity, a certainty, and something that must be done." When we see "must" used in this context it means that it is not optional. Here the word "must" is expressing that in spirit and in truth is the only way to acceptably worship God.[55]

God seeks true worshippers. Those individuals are those who "worship Him in spirit and in truth." To worship God in spirit means that it must be done from the heart. To worship God in truth means that it must be done according as God has specified in the Bible. Worshipping God in spirit and in truth is a matter that must not be taken lightly. It is serious business. If we have any regard for the well being of our own souls, we should be sure we are worshipping God in spirit and in truth.

Worship is a time when we show deep, sincere respect and love to the Creator.[56] God is the one who holds our eternal destiny in His hands. Our salvation is a very serious matter and it doesn't just happen. We must work it out daily "with fear and trembling."[57] Our salvation rests on whether our worship is pleasing to God or not. On Judgment Day, we will stand before God Almighty and have to answer the question, 'What did you do with what I gave you?' At that point, there won't be any time for corrections.

God does not need to have our worship, but we must worship Him to please Him. We worship through singing, praying, studying His word, giving, and communion. We express our worship in different ways in order to bring us closer to God and to cause us to think more like Him, and thus, becoming more like Him.[58] Our worship not only honors and magnifies God, but it is also for our own edification and strength.

Worship helps us develop a Christ-like character. We become like those we admire and worship. When we worship God we tend to value what God values and gradually take on the characteristics and qualities of God, but we never attain to His level.[59] How do we take on the mind of Christ?[60] Our mind is renewed as we study and meditate on God's word and worship Him.[61] We should always bring our very best in worship to God and for it is prescribed by Him in the Bible.[62] The Christian's worship is of the greatest importance.

STUDY GOALS

Goals for this lesson:

1. Learn how to please God through worshipping Him

2. Gain a deeper understanding of what it means to worship

3. Incorporate worship principles in your life daily

4. Draw nearer to God through regular worship

DIGGING IN DEEPER

What do the following Bible verses reveal to us about our worship? Please read each passage below, provide a detailed explanation, and share your thoughts with the group.

Romans 12:1

John 4:24

James 1:27

John 4:23

Exodus 20:4

John 4:20

John 4:21

Job 1:21

Hebrews 10:1

Exodus 20:5

PRAYER & ACCOUNTABILITY CHECK IN

1. Are you comfortable with how you worship God? Could you be freer with your worship?

2. What makes you uncomfortable with taking your worship to the next level? Explain.

3. Do you lead your family in worshipping God or do you allow them to grow on their own? Do you model worship for your family? Spouse? Children? Other loved ones? Explain.

4. Is there anything in your life hindering you from being a true worshipper of God? Explain.

5. Pray and ask God to help you be better at worshipping Him. Ask him to help you with things that hinder a deeper level of worship. Pray for His direction, discernment, guidance, and wisdom.

GROUP DISCUSSION

Take a look at the passages below and try to determine what God's Word reveals about our worship of God.

1. Does God resist the humble, obedient, and proud? (James 4:6, 10)

2. Why does God want us to be humble.

3. How is God to be worshipped? (John 4:23-24)

4. Will God accept our worship even though it is not in spirit and in truth if we are sincere? Explain.

5. Who is to direct our ways in religion? (Jeremiah 10:23)

(Circle One) God? What the majority believes? The preacher?

6. Is God the only one who has the right to determine how we are to worship Him? Explain.

7. Who should we worship? (Acts 17:24-25)

(Circle One) Nature, since we evolved from nature?

God who gave us life and breath and made all things?

Mankind, since man has become so great?

8. How are we to work out our own salvation? (Philippians 2:12)

(Circle One) With fear and trembling?

Any way we want to?

Let the church do it for me?

9. Why must we be concerned about our eternal destiny?

10. If we draw near to God what will happen? (James 4:8)

(Circle One) He will not draw near to us?

He will move away from us?

He will draw near to us?

11. Why does God want us to draw nearer to Him?

12. Whose mind should we try to imitate? (Philippians 2:5)

(Circle One) The mind of some famous person such as the president of our country?

The mind of Christ?

We should develop our own mind the way we want?

13. Why should we imitate the mind of Christ?

14. How do we not become conformed to this world? (Romans 12:2)

(Circle One) By the renewing of our mind as we study and meditate on God's word?

By being a rebel?

There is no way to keep from being conformed to this world.

15. Why should we not be conformed to this world?

16. What should we set our minds on? (Colossians 3:2)

(Circle One) Getting rich? Having fun? Things in heaven?

17. Why should we not set our mind on things on the earth?

MEMORIZATION VERSE

"Exalt the Lord our God and worship at his holy mountain, for the Lord our God is holy."[63]

KeyPoints

1. God is seeking true worshippers who worship Him in spirit and truth.

2. We worship God by exalting Him and showing Him deep love and respect.

3. God wants us to worship Him with all of our mind, soul, body, and strength.

Lifelines

1. Make sure that at least one person will be praying for you during the week and will hold you accountable for something that you have shared.

2. Regularly review and memorize important scripture passages about worship.

3. Review the Accountability Questions in this study guide as needed.

4. Ask God to give you wisdom about how you can be a true worshipper.

GROUP EXERCISES

1. What are your greatest challenges with respect to worship? Share your challenges with the group. What do you suppose those who don't share your same challenges have, or do, or get that you don't?

2. Using your Notes Pages, list several key strategies that will help you be a better worshipper. Discuss your strategies with the group and allow them to give you feedback about your idea(s). Each member should take a turn sharing and letting the group critique his or her idea(s).

3. Locate and share with the group some scripture verses that are helpful to you regarding worship. Each person in the group should commit at least one verse to memory.

4. Individual Exercise: Make up a prayer list (write it on your Note Pages) for the areas where you struggle in worship. To the extent you feel comfortable, share those areas with the group.

5. Individual Exercise: Share with the group some books and resources that you have found helpful to supplement your Bible reading. To the extent you are able, locate some new tools to help enhance your daily Christian life.

LEADERS PRAY REGULARLY

STUDY START

"This then, is how you should pray: 'Our Father in heaven, hallowed be your name, your kingdom come, your will be done, on earth as it is in heaven. Give us today our daily bread....'"[64]

In Luke 11:1 Jesus' disciples asked, "Lord, teach us to pray."[65] Many Christians today need to learn to pray. People who are new in the faith may have never studied about prayer. Some members do not pray regularly so they may not know all the things they can pray about. Some may pray regularly, but aren't familiar with what the Bible says about how to pray. All of us can improve in this aspect of worship. We need to learn more about prayer so we will know what to pray about so that we can experience the power of God answering our prayers.

A. We Should Praise God's Character and Work.

Jesus began the model prayer by praising God's name.[66] Many psalms are filled with praise (i.e., Psalm 86:5-12).[67] We should pray to God and praise Him. Review the following passages and consider some particular qualities or works of God that were praised in prayer.

1 Chronicles 29:10-13. [Psalm 86:8-10; Neh. 9:4-6; 1 Kings 8:23; 2 Kings 19:15; Matt. 6:13; Rev 11:17; 2 Sam. 7:22].[68]

1 Chronicles 29:11,12. [Jer. 32:16-23; Eph. 1:16-19; Job 42:1,2; Neh. 9:4-38; Dan. 2:20-23]; Psalm 86:5-12 (note v5). [Psalm 143:1-12; 1 Sam. 2:2].[69]

Psalm 86:5. [Col. 1:12-14; 2 Sam. 7:23; Neh. 9:4-38; Luke 2:37,38; 1 Kings 8:23; Ezra 9:8,9; Psalm 17:7].[70]

Jeremiah 32:16-23 (note v19). [Dan. 2:20-23; 1 Sam. 2:3]; Jeremiah 32:19,23. [1 Sam. 2:6-10; Gen. 18:25; Psalm 90:7-11].[71]

Psalm 90:1-4. [Psalm 102:1,12,24-27]; Nehemiah 9:4-8. [Neh. 1:5; 1 Kings 8:23-30; Dan. 9:4; Psalm 143:1]; Nehemiah 9:4-6. [Jer. 32:17; Psalm 90:2; 102:1,24,25; 2 Kings 19:15; Acts 4:24; 1 Sam. 2:6].[72]

B. We Should Pray on Behalf of Others.

    1 Timothy 2:1,2 says to offer prayer, supplication, intercession, and giving of thanks on behalf of all men.[73] Yet we sometimes neglect to pray for others because we concentrate so much on our own interests. Please review the scripture passages below and try to determine some groups of people for whom we should pray.

1 Timothy 2:1,2. [Ezra 6:10; 1 Chron. 29:19]; 1 Chron. 29:19. [Matthew 19:13-15; Gen. 25:21,22; 24:12-14; 18:23-33; 1 Sam. 1:10-12; 2 Sam. 12:15,16; Luke 1:13]; Romans 10:1-3. [Matt. 9:36-38; Luke 23:34; Acts 7:60].[74]

Luke 6:27,28. [Acts 7:60; Luke 23:34]; 3 John 2; James 5:16; Num. 11:2; 2 Sam. 12:15,16; Gen. 20:17,18.[75]

Ephesians 6:18-20; Col. 4:3,4; Acts 4:25-29; 6:6; 14:23; 13:3; 1 Thess. 5:25; Matt. 9:36-38; 2 Thess. 3:1,2; Heb. 13:18]; Ephesians 6:18; James 5:16.

C. We Should Make Requests and Give Thanks

We should pray for the things we truly need, however some people forget to thank God for what they have received. Their prayers consist almost entirely of asking for more. God is a generous God, willing to give us what we need. But He also expects appreciation for what He gives. Review the scripture passages below to learn about how we can make requests and give thanks.

Passages teaching we can request what we need

Philippians 4:6,7[76]

Matthew 7:7-11[77]

1 Peter 5:7[78]

James 4:2,3[79]

1 John 5:14,15[80]

Passages teaching we should also give thanks for our blessings

Philippians 4:6,7[81]

1Timothy 2:1[82]

Ephesians 5:20[83]

D. Some Specific Things We Should Pray About

A close examination of Bible prayers can teach us the kind of specific things that are commonly included in Bible prayers. We may pray about these things for ourselves or for others. We may request them and should give thanks when we receive them. Review the scripture passages below of things we can pray specifically about.

God's will to be done - Matthew 6:9-13 (note v10). [Matt. 26:39]; *Necessities of life* - Matthew 6:11. [Acts 27:35; Matt. 15:36; 14:19; 1 Tim. 4:3-5; Luke 24:30]; *Forgiveness of sins* and deliverance from the consequences of sin - Matthew 6:12.

Ability to recognize and resist temptation - Matthew 6:13. [Matt. 26:41; Eph. 6:11-18; 2 Cor. 13:7; Luke 22:31,32; John 17:14-16]; *Good health* and freedom from other threats to life or safety - 3 John 2; 2 Kings 20:1-7 (Hezekiah) [James 5:13-18; 2 Cor.

12:7-10; 1 Kings 8:35-53; 2 Chron. 7:13-15; Jonah 2:1-10; Psalm 50:15; 86:6,7; 32:6,7; 2 Sam. 12:15,16; Num. 11:2; Luke 21:36].

Deliverance from enemies and persecution - Acts 12:1,5,12. [2 Thess. 3:1,2; 2 Cor. 1:8-11; Acts 4:23-31; 16:25; 1 Kings 8:33-35; 2 Kings 19:4,15-19] *Freedom from oppression by rulers* - 1 Timothy 2:1,2. [Neh. 1:11-2:5]; *Safety in travel and care for loved ones we are separated from* - Acts 21:5. [Acts 20:36-38; 28:15; Ezra 8:21-23; Gen. 24:26,27; 1 Thess. 3:9-11; 2 Tim. 1:3-5; Rom. 1:10; 15:30-32; Philem. 22].

Peace, courage, joy instead of disappointment or discouragement - Philippians 4:6,7. [1 Samuel 8:6-9; 2:1-11; Jer. 29:7; Psalm 122:6; 1 Peter 5:7; Matt. 26:36-46; Col. 1:11; 1 Thess. 3:9; 2 Sam. 7:18-29]; *Knowledge, wisdom, and understanding of God's will* - Psalm 119:169-172. Note that this comes today through the Scriptures, not by direct revelation. [James 1:5,6; Col. 1:9,10; Phil. 1:9,10; Psalm 86:6,11; 143:1,8,10].

Salvation of lost sinners - Romans 10:1-3. [Luke 23:34; Acts 7:60]; *Laborers to teach the lost* - Matthew 9:36-38; *Bold, clear preaching* - Ephesians 6:18-20. [Col. 4:3,4]; *Opportunities to preach and teach* - Colossians 4:3 [2 Thess. 3:1]; *Support for preachers* - Philippians 1:3-5; *Choosing of elders, deacons, teachers,* etc. - Acts 14:23. [Acts 6:6; 13:3]; *Jesus' death, the Lord's supper* - Matthew 26:26-29. [1 Cor. 11:23-26]; *Baptism* - Luke 3:21.

Faithfulness, good works, a life pleasing to God - Philippians 1:3-6,9-11. [Col. 1:9-11; 4:12; John 17:9-12; 1 Thess. 3:10-13; 2 Thess. 1:11]; *Love* - Philippians 1:9. [1 Thess. 3:10-12; Eph. 3:14-19]; *Strength* - Colossians 1:9-11. [Eph. 3:14-19; 2 Thess. 1:11].

Patience, long-suffering - Colossians 1:11; *Grace and mercy* - 2 Corinthians 4:15. [Psalm 4:1; 86:3-6; 1 Cor. 1:4];

Proper speech - Psalm 141:1-3; ***Sanctification*** - John 17:17; ***Unity*** - John 17:20-23; ***Eternal life, eternal glory*** - John 17:24-26.

This list is not comprehensive, but it suggests many things we could properly pray for. Remember that these are things both to make request for and to give thanks for. Also note how Bible prayers often concerned spiritual needs and blessings. Some people seem to view prayer like sending a "Christmas list" to Santa Claus for all the physical things they want. Biblical prayers may concern physical needs, but mainly they reflect man's greatest needs which are spiritual.

STUDY GOALS

Goals for this lesson:

1. Learn different ways we can pray and connect with God

2. Gain a deeper understanding of the meaning of prayer

3. Incorporate more specific prayer practices in your life

4. Draw nearer to God through regular prayer

5. Learn about praying for spiritual needs and blessings

DIGGING DEEPER

Look up and review each passage below and try to determine what God's Word reveals about prayer.

1. How Often Should We Pray

1 Corinthians 1:4

Ephesians 6:18

Philippians 1:3-4

Colossians 1:3

1 Thessalonians 5:17

2. How Should We Pray?

Psalm 66:17

Psalm 95:2

Matthew 6:9-13

1 Corinthians 14:15

James 1:6

3. What Should We Pray For?

Psalm 50:14-15

Psalm 118:25

Psalm 122:6

Romans 10:1

Romans 10:13

4. Who Should We Pray For?

Romans 15:30

2 Corinthians 1:11

1 Timothy 2:1-2

James 5:13-14

James 5:16

PRAYER & ACCOUNTABILITY CHECK-IN

1. Do you pray regularly? Do you submit all of your thoughts and ideas to God everyday? How often do you pray?

2. Do you view prayer as an obligation or an act of worship? Explain.

3. Do you lead your family in prayer? How often do you pray together as a family? What does your family time with God look like? Explain.

4. Is there anything in your life hindering you from being more effective in prayer? Individually or leading your family? If so, explain, and if you feel comfortable share it with the group.

5. Pray and ask God to help you with your personal prayer life. Ask him to help you with those things that hinder your prayers. Pray specifically for God's direction, discernment, guidance, and wisdom.

GROUP DISCUSSION

1. Is there a particular passage or verse in Scripture that has helped you understand prayer or what it means to pray? Explain.

2. Make a list of how you pray (i.e., when, where, etc.) and share it with your group. What is your favorite way to pray? Why?

3. Name some important examples of prayer that we can follow from the pages of Scripture. Share them with the group. How are you following biblical examples of prayer in your life? Can you be better? If so, how?

4. Share one or two stories about how prayer has changed your life. How has God answered prayer in your life? Explain.

5. How can you improve your daily prayer life?

6. Did you learn something new in this study about prayer that you didn't know before? How much time do you spend praying each day? week? Month? If applicable, can you give God more time?

MEMORIZATION VERSE

Let us come into his presence with thanksgiving; let us make a joyful noise to him with songs of praise![84]

KeyPoints

1. God wants us to connect with Him through a regular prayer life.

2. We can take all of our cares and concerns to the Lord and trust that He hears us.

3. God wants us to be specific in our prayers for the needs of other people.

Lifelines

1. Make sure that at least one person will be praying for you during the week and will hold you accountable for something that you have shared.

2. Regularly review and memorize important scripture passages about prayer.

3. Review the Accountability Questions in this study guide as needed.

4. Ask God to give you wisdom about how you can be more diligent in prayer.

GROUP EXERCISES

1. What are your greatest challenges with regard to maintaining a regular prayer life? Share your challenges with the group. What do you suppose those who struggle less in this area of life have, or do, or get that you don't?

2. Using your Note Pages, make a list of your struggle areas with regard to prayer. Write down some key strategies that can help you overcome the tendency towards not praying as you ought to.

3. Locate and share with the group some scripture verses that are helpful to you with respect to prayer. Each person in the group should commit at least one verse to memory.

4. Individual Exercise: Review the Accountability Questions in the back of this book and be honest in your responses. Examine yourself and to the extent you feel comfortable sharing with the group.

5. Individual Exercise: Share with the group some books and resources that you have found helpful to supplement your Bible reading on prayer. To the extent you are able, locate some new tools to help enhance your daily Christian life.

RESOURCES

PRAYER NOTES

_____

_____

_____

_____

_____

_____

_____

_____

_____

_____

_____

_____

_____

_____

_____

_____

PRAYER NOTES

PRAYER NOTES

PRAYER NOTES

ACCOUNTABILITY NOTES

ACCOUNTABILITY NOTES

_____

_____

_____

_____

_____

_____

_____

_____

_____

_____

_____

_____

_____

_____

_____

_____

ACCOUNTABILITY NOTES

ACCOUNTABILITY NOTES

ACCOUNTABILITY QUESTIONS

1. Have you spent time alone with God on a regular basis? Are you satisfied with the amount of time you have spent?

2. How much time did you spend in prayer this week? Are you satisfied with the amount of time you have spent?

3. What one sin plagued your walk with God this week? Did you pray for other people?

4. Did you worship in church this week? Did you serve in church this week?

5. Did you study and meditate on God's Word? What did you learn? What passages and topics did you read? What is God trying to teach you?

6. Did you accomplish your spiritual goals this week? What do you see as your number one goal for next week?

7. Are you giving to the Lord's work financially? Are you giving more than you are receiving?

8. How have you demonstrated a servant's heart? What is your main prayer request for this week?

9. Are you growing deeper in your spiritual walk? Are you investing in time alone with God?

10. Have you been studying the Bible everyday? Do you spend adequate time in prayer and Bible study?

11. Do you need to confess any sin? Are you living according to God's plan and purpose for your life?

12. What has God been speaking into your life? What is God trying to show you about your walk with Him?

13. Have you been a good spiritual leader in your family? Church? Work? Community?

14. How have you experienced God in your life this week? Have you had an encounter with God?

15. Are you giving a regular tithe to the local church? Do you tithe regularly? Have you ever given above and beyond your regular tithe?

16. Are you using your power for the glory of God alone? Do you trust the Holy Spirit to work on your behalf in every area of your life?

17. Are you fulfilling the mandates of your calling? Are you making an impact while you are here on earth? Do you understand your purpose?

18. Do you have private worship time with God? Do you worship Him in spirit and truth?

19. Are you growing in your daily dependence on God? Do you believe that God can do beyond what you can ask or think?

20. Have you lied in response to any of these questions? Is it possible for you to be an effective leader if you are not honest with yourself?

NOTES

1. See Romans 12:6-8;1 Chronicles 12:27, 13:1; 2 Chronicles 32:21; Isaiah 9:16, 55:4; and Matthew 15:14.
2. John 10:11. (NIV)
3. Ibid.
4. 1 Corinthians 11:1. (NIV)
5. The Bible provides us with numerous references concerning leading by example. Some passages are as follows: 1 Peter 5:2, 5:3; 1 Corinthians 11:1, Philippians 3:17, Acts 20:28, Ephesians 4:11-16, Titus 2:1-10, Romans 12:1. These passages help us understand the characteristics we must possess to be servant leaders, but the best example to follow is Jesus Christ.
6. Deuteronomy 8:3. (NIV)
7. Ezekiel 34:16. (NIV)
8. Proverbs 3:12. (NIV)
9. Galatians 6:2. (NIV)
10. Matthew 7:15. (NIV)
11. John 14:6. (NIV)
12. John 13. (NIV)
13. Proverbs 3:5. (NIV)
14. Jeremiah 29:11. (NIV)
15. Romans 12:1. (NIV)
16. Romans 12:1:6-8. (NIV)
17. John 10:11. (NIV)
18. As a personal point of reference, one of my favorite verses is: "Be joyful always; pray continually; give thanks in all

circumstances, for this is God's will for you in Christ Jesus."1 Thessalonians 5:16-18 (NIV)

19. Hebrews 4:12. (NASB)

20. Matthew 4:4. (NIV)

21. 2 Peter 1:20. (NIV)

22. John 6:63. (NIV)

23. Hebrews 4:12. (NASB); John 6:63. (NIV)

24. 2 Timothy 3:16. (NIV)

25. Hebrews 5:14. (NIV)

26. Ephesians 4:11-16. (NIV)

27. Matthew 10:30; Luke 2:7. (NIV)

28. Kaiser, Walter and Moises, Silva, *An Introduction to Biblical Hermeneutics*, Zondervan, 1994.

29. Kaiser, Walter and Moises, Silva, *An Introduction to Biblical Hermeneutics*, Zondervan, 1994; Klein, William W. and Blomberg, Craig, and Hubbard, Robert, *Introduction to Biblical Interpretation*, Word, 1993.

30. Ibid.

31. Hebrews 4:12. (NASB)

32. Mark 10:45. (NIV)

33. 1 Peter 4:10-11. (NIV)

34. Ibid.

35. Romans 12:1-2. (NIV)

36. Ibid.

37. Romans 12:1-2. (NIV)

38. Mark 10:45. (NIV)

39. 2 Corinthians 9:6-7. (NIV)

40. Psalm 50:10. (NIV)

41. John 3:27. (NASB)

42. Luke 6:38. (KJV)

43. 1 Corinthians 16:1-2. (NIV)

44. Ibid.

45. 2 Corinthians 8:12. (NIV)

46. Matthew 6:19-21. (NASB)

47. 2 Corinthians 9:6-7. (NIV)

48. Matthew 6:1-4. (NASB)

49. Romans 12:1. (KJV)

50. 2 Corinthians 9:6-7. (NIV)

51. Hebrews 13:15. (NIV)

52. James 4:6,10 tells us that God resists the proud, but gives grace to the humble. Humble yourselves in the sight of the Lord, and He will lift you up. James 4:6,10. (NASB)

53. Jesus says in John 4:23-24, "But the hour is coming, and now is, when true worshippers will worship the Father in spirit and in truth, for such the Father seeks to worship Him. God is spirit and those who worship him must worship in spirit and truth." John 4:23-24. (RSV)

54. Ibid.

55. John 4:23-24. (NIV)

56. Acts 17:24-25 says, "God who made the world and all thing in it, since He is Lord of heaven and earth, does not dwell in temples made with hands; nor is He served by human hands, as though He needed anything, since He Himself gives life and breath and all things." Acts 17:24-25. (NASB)

57. Philippians 2:12 tells us to, "work out your own salvation with fear and trembling." Philippians 2:12. (RSV)

58. James 4:8 tells us to, "Draw near to God and He will draw near to you." James 4:8. (NASB)

59. As Philippians 2:5 says, "Let this mind be in you which was also in Christ." Philippians 2:5. (KJV)

60. In Romans 12:2 we read, "Do not be conformed to this world,

but be transformed by the renewal of your mind." Romans 12:2. (RSV)

61. When we worship God we develop such traits as forgiveness, tenderness, justice, righteousness, purity, kindness, and love. All of this is preparing us for eternal life in heaven with God and Christ. As we are told in Colossians 3:2, "Set your mind on things above, not on the things that are on the earth." Colossians 3:2. (NASB)

62. As we worship God, we give Him ourselves. Romans 12:1 says, "I beseech you therefore, brethren, by the mercies of God, that ye present your bodies a living sacrifice, holy, acceptable unto God which is your reasonable service." Romans 12:1. (KJV) We must do our very best everyday. Jesus tells us in Matthew 22:37, "Love the Lord your God with all your heart and all your soul and all your mind." Matthew 22:37. (NASB) All our heart, soul, and mind, or in other words, our total being must be in our worship.

63. Psalm 99:9. (NIV)

64. Matthew 6:9-13. (NIV)

65. Luke 11:1. (NIV)

66. Matthew 6:9. (NIV)

67. Note Psalm 86:5-12. (NIV)

68. These passages reveal God's authority and Lordship. He is the true God, in contrast to idols.

69. God's power, God's holiness, goodness, and righteousness.

70. God's mercy, grace, kindness, and willingness to forgive. God has provided redemption and salvation for His people, especially sending Jesus as our Savior.

71. These passages reveal God's wisdom, knowledge, and justice. God cares for His people and rewards them but punishes the wicked.

72. God's eternal existence, faithfulness to His word, and His work as the Creator and Source of life.

73. These passages reveal that we should pray for rulers, children family members, and lost sinners. Remember, however, that these people must meet the gospel conditions of salvation in order to be forgiven.

74. Enemies, persecutors, the sick and suffering.

75. Elders, deacons, preachers, and teachers, and all Christians.

76. Instead of worrying, let your requests be made known to God. The word "supplication" refers to requests for needs to be supplied.

77. God is like a loving father who gives what his children need. If we ask, we will receive.

78. Cast your cares on God because He cares for you.

79. Sometimes we do not receive because we do not ask. On the other hand, God will not answer selfish requests for things we do not need.

80. If we ask according to God's will, we receive our petitions. (Cf. 1 John 3:21,22; John 14:13,14; 15:7,16; 16:23,24,26). (NIV)

81. Our requests should be made known with thanksgiving.

82. Prayers for others should include thanksgiving.

83. We should give thanks to the Father always for all things. (1 Thess. 5:18; Col. 4:2; 2:7; 3:17)

BIBLIOGRAPHY

Bible Study

Traina, Robert, *Methodical Bible Study*, Zondervan Publishing (1980)

Fee, Gordan and Stuart, Douglas, *How to Read the Bible for All its Worth*, 3rd edition, Zondervan Publishing (2003)

Fee, Gordan and Stuart, Douglas, *How to Read the Bible Book by Book*, Zondervan Publishing (2002)

Stein, Robert, *A Basic Guide to Interpreting the Bible*, Baker Books (1994)

Prayer

Pritchard, John, *How to Pray: A Practical Handbook*, The Cromwell Press (2004)

Gale, Stanley, *Why Do We Pray?*, P&R Publishing (2012)

Stanley, Charles, *The Ultimate Conversation: Talking with God Through Prayer*, Howard Books (2013)

Worship

Carson, D.A., *Worship by the Book*, Zondervan (2002)

Killinger, John, *Lost in Wonder, Love Praise: Prayers for Christian Worship*, Abingdon Press (2011)

Carson, D.A., *Worship: Adoration and Action*, W & S Publishers (1992)

Leadership

Lewis, Rick, *Mentoring Matters: Building Strong Christian Leaders, Avoiding Burnout, and Reaching the Finish Line*, Monarch Books (2009)

Michael, Larry, *Spurgeon on Leadership: Key Insights for Christian Leaders*, Kregal Academic & Professional (2010)

Evans, Tony, *Kingdom Man*, Tyndale House Publishers (2013)

Serving

Swindoll, Charles, *Improve Your Serve*, W Publishing Group (1981)

Searcy, Nelson, *The Greatness Principle*, Baker Book House (2012)

Giving

Alcorn, Randy, *The Treasure Principle*, Multnomah Publishers (2005)

Stott, John, *The Grace of Giving*, Hendrickson Publishers (2012)

Burkett, Larry, *Giving & Tithing*, Moody Publishers (1998)

CPSIA information can be obtained at www.ICGtesting.com
Printed in the USA
LVOW13s0018171013

357248LV00002B/2/P